50 NOT OUT
LOCOMOTIVES WORKING AFTER HALF A CENTURY

John Jackson

AMBERLEY

First published 2018

Amberley Publishing
The Hill, Stroud
Gloucestershire, GL5 4EP

www.amberley-books.com

ISBN 978 1 4456 7594 7 (print)
ISBN 978 1 4456 7595 4 (ebook)

British Library Cataloguing in Publication Data.
A catalogue record for this book is available from
the British Library.

Origination by Amberley Publishing.
Printed in the UK.

Introduction

How many times have we heard the phrase 'they don't make 'em like they used to'? Whatever the merits or otherwise of applying such a comment to UK railway locomotives, the fact remains that there are many longstanding survivors from our railway past.

Of course, we all know of the valuable role played by preserved railways in the UK. They have secured a place in history for heritage diesel and electric locos, as well as many steam examples. But diesel and electric examples from a number of ageing loco classes still remain on rail operators' books, and many are over half a century old. A quick tally suggests that locos from around a dozen classes survive. They continue to attract more than their fair share of interest, particularly among the nostalgia enthusiast market. While some are sidelined, many still see day-to-day service in the hands of mainstream operators.

To use a cricketing expression, these locos are '50 not out'. That is to say, they have notched up a half century. What's more, having passed that milestone, they are, or at least until recently were, still going strong in good working order. Between 100 and 200 individual examples remain '50 not out' on the network. This book is, then, a photographic selection of many of these veteran locos that can still be seen around our network today.

I frequently get a glimpse of one of these veteran machines when passing Derby. While it might not see regular use these days, Class 73 locomotive No. 73101 still rests alongside the main line here. In Pullman livery and named *The Royal Alex*, this machine holds a special place in my own enthusiast memories. Back on the morning of 18 July 1968 as E6007, this loco worked light engine through Northampton station. To my amazement, E6007– the first of the batch to be built at the Vulcan Foundry – was heading to Crewe for tyre turning. It remains one of my most exciting sightings through my home town in over half a century.

Talking of nostalgia, most enthusiasts both young and old have a soft spot for the Class 37 locomotive. This is due, in part, to the sound that has given them the affectionate nickname of 'tractors'. Many examples of these popular

English Electric-built Type 3 locos can still be seen across large parts of the UK railways and their duties are diverse. They can still be found working the nuclear flask traffic centred on Sellafield and loco-hauled passenger services in both Cumbria and East Anglia. They are also mainstays on Network Rail Test Train services, often covering significant distances on forays from the Derby operations base. Four examples were re-designated as Class 97 for specific use with Network Rail operations. The surviving Class 37s have outlasted many more recently built classes, and some by a considerable number of years. There are many more active Class 37s in regular use than their Class 60 counterparts for example. This is despite the latter class having been built as recently as the late 1980s and early 1990s.

The 37s are but one example, though. The Class 73 is another. These electro-diesels can be seen literally from one end of the country to the other. They can be found in use with GBRf in Kent and along the South Coast of England and on ScotRail sleeper duties across Scotland. Again, several class members are regular performers on Network Rail duties, bringing examples to other parts of the country, particularly to and from Network Rail's Derby base.

The variety of locos is perhaps surprising. This book demonstrates the diversity of classes that have passed their half century and remain 'not out', focusing on locomotives still seeing use on the main UK rail network rather than on preserved lines. This book also includes a few examples of locos that are privately owned but certified for 'main line use'. I have to confess to being extremely pleasantly surprised, and delighted, when, back in 2013, GBRf commandeered a Class 52 Western to work at their Wellingborough yard, close to my home! Sadly, I am afraid there is no photograph of the Western. However, I hope the variety of motive power grouped here gives you the chance to wander down memory lane.

So, let's step back half a century or more for a moment. The 1960s saw the biggest shake up on the railway network with the swift elimination of steam locomotives in favour of diesel and electric power. A large number of different loco classes emerged during this period of transition. Some fell by the wayside almost immediately while others withstood the test of time.

The locomotive products on offer came from a variety of different manufacturers and, inevitably, only a few of these companies' offerings have survived until the present day.

As a youngster I watched the gradual electrification of the West Coast Main Line (WCML) and witnessed the elimination of steam traction. They were to be replaced on express passenger services out of Euston by the Class 40 diesel locos and, soon afterwards, they were in turn replaced by Class 86 electric traction. Little did I know that, although the Class 40s have gone, many Class 86 examples would survive and make it into my '50 not out club'. These electric locos can still be found working Freightliner's container trains, in pairs, on the West Coast Main Line. Their use extends from the London suburbs northwards to the Central Scotland container hub at Coatbridge.

Much of the freight traffic that remains on today's railways has changed significantly over the years. The trains themselves tend not to be joined or split within the many yards that were once dotted across the country for this purpose. The last few years have therefore seen a dramatic reduction in the demand for so-called shunting locos that used to be linked to these train moves.

As a result, the majority of the once substantial fleet of Class 08 and Class 09 diesel shunters have been scrapped or sidelined. Originally introduced in the early 1950s, ten years later, when the final deliveries had been made, class numbers had reached well in excess of a thousand. But, as this book highlights, some working examples can still be found around the country. DB Cargo, in particular, has more recently used the much younger, and more powerful, Class 60 and Class 66 examples for shunting purposes, where such a need still exists.

There are no photographs of Class 60s or 66s to be found here, however. They date from the late 1980s and the late 1990s respectively, and it remains to be seen whether they will eventually become '50 not out'.

But there are still plenty of examples of other classes to be found in this collection. Two of the major operators in particular, DRS and GBRf, still make regular use of these older machines. The Class 20s find themselves active employment on London Underground stock movements as well as, at least until 2017, working railhead treatment trains in connection with the leaf-fall season in autumn. Each year we hear speculation that 'this year will be their last'.

The Brush Type 4 machines are another class that soldiers on. Once numbering well over 500 locos, some Class 47s survive along with their Class 57 'derivatives'. They carry a range of liveries and colours, too. As I write this, Colas have sold their survivors to GBRf. Furthermore, there is speculation that at least one will be outshopped in Caledonian Sleeper colours. These GBRf machines already see action on empty stock moves of these sleeper coaches.

Further south, the Class 57 examples can be found strategically placed on the WCML while performing their 'Thunderbird' rescue duties in support of Virgin Trains. Other examples are to be found in the small dedicated pool for working the six-nights-a-week sleeper services between London Paddington and the West of England in both directions.

Veteran machines are also used by the West Coast Railway Company; indeed, its core business is built around the use of veteran diesel (and steam) locomotives as motive power on its charter trains. In addition to those classes already mentioned, their remaining Class 33 machines sometimes get an outing.

In addition to GBRf's random use of a Western Class 52, several Class 50s are finding a new lease of life employed on main line duties.

The Rail Operations Group (ROG) was announced as the 2017 UK Rail Operator of the Year. They have no day-to-day involvement in running passenger, freight or Network Rail related civil engineer's trains; rather, their focus is on the movement of rolling stock around the country. ROG's dedicated fleet of locos, chiefly comprising Classes 37 and 47, all qualify for my '50 not out club'. Their locos can be seen right across the country, often benefiting from recent loco adaptations. This means that they are not reliant on the more expensive use of barrier or translator wagons involved in stock movements such as electric multiple units (EMUs). Several such examples are included here. Their locos are also used for one-off loco movements on behalf of other owners.

In fact, as I hope is demonstrated in the pages of this book, there are still a considerable variety of '50 not out' locomotives to be found on the UK railway today. On the pages that follow, there are close to 200 examples from a variety of operators, across a range of loco classes, captured across the full length of this country. To put the age of these 'heritage' machines into perspective, almost all pre-date England's 1966 World Cup win and the following year's worldwide 'Summer of Love'. The fact that I can remember both shows my age, too!

Space precludes the inclusion of the full loco history of numbers, owners and liveries, etc., but I have added their original numbers and approximate dates of birth. For the younger readers, the original numbering system for all the locos featured in this book pre-dates the introduction of TOPS (Total Operations Processing Systems) numbering in 1973. That system is still in use today. Prior to that date, the enthusiast had to be satisfied with the D (diesel) and E (electric) numbers shown throughout this book.

As always, I hope you enjoy your journey browsing through these pages as much as I have enjoyed compiling them!

John Jackson

Direct Rail Services (DRS) continues to use a number of loco types that qualify for inclusion in this book. In particular, its popular Class 20s have been brought out of storage to provide additional options during the leaf-fall season. On 25 October 2017, No. 20312 leads a railhead treatment train through Hatfield & Stainforth. Numbered D8042 when new, this loco was built in November 1959. Despite withdrawal and subsequent reinstatement to traffic, it is not far short of sixty years old.

No. 20312's partner on this date was sister loco No. 20305 *Gresty Bridge*. A comparative youngster, this loco was originally numbered D8095 when built in October 1961. This railhead treatment train was on a circuitous diagram between Grimsby Town and Bridlington, helping the rail network contend with autumn leaves and the residue they leave on the tracks.

West Coast Railway Company (WCRC) maintains a fleet of heritage locomotives, including several examples of Class 37 locos. Dating back to the end of 1962 and then numbered D6786, one such example is No. 37516 *Loch Laddon*. It is seen at Inverness on 13 May 2014 shortly before leading a rake of WCRC empty coaching stock south to Aviemore.

Another WCRC Class 37 working in Scotland saw the use of No. 37669 on 8 October 2017. This loco was delivered new in March 1963 as D6829. This time the location is the remote West Highland Line outpost of Rannoch. No. 37669 is seen leaving the station heading south on the rear of a return charter train having made an extended stop here while working from Fort William to Kettering. A shot of the leading loco (No. 47804) on this charter is included later in this book.

While the majority of locos featured in this publication operate on diesel power, Freightliner still operates a small fleet of sixteen Class 86 electric locomotives. Dating back to the mid-1960s, they were numbered in the E3101 to E3200 range when new. Today these locos are chiefly found operating in pairs along the length of the West Coast Main Line (WCML), hauling container trains. One such combination is the pairing of No. 86610 (built September 1965 as E3104) and No. 86637 (built December 1965 as E3130) on 9 April 2015. The pair are seen waiting for the signal from Carlisle station. They are on a southbound Freightliner container working from Coatbridge to Crewe.

Further south on the WCML on 29 September 2017, No. 86607 is captured at Bletchley (with No. 86622 for company) on a southbound Freightliner from Crewe to Felixstowe. The pair will be replaced by diesel power at Ipswich for the train's run down the non-electrified branch from there to the Suffolk port. Both locos were built in August 1965, No. 86607 as E3176 and No. 86622 as E3174.

Over a ten-year period in the 1950s and early 1960s, around 1,000 examples of what were to become Class 08 and Class 09 diesel shunters were built for general shunting duties. Today their numbers have dwindled as demands for shunting any sort of rolling stock have reduced dramatically. DB Cargo has completely dispensed with their use. On 16 May 2015, two EWS-branded examples, No. 08738 (built in 1960 as D3906) and No. 08630 (built in 1959 as D3797), are found at their Toton base, awaiting their disposal.

This 1956-built example still sees use shunting at Electro Motive's base at Longport, near Stoke-on-Trent. On 22 September 2017, No. 08220 (originally numbered D3290) is glimpsed from a passing train. It still carries BR blue livery.

The Class 73 electro-diesels are another example of a class that has survived from the 1960s to the present day. Around thirty examples from the original fleet of forty-nine locos can still be found across the network. They were built with the Southern Region in mind and were capable of taking power either from the third rail or their diesel engines. Although their range still extends as far north as Scotland (on sleeper services), Tonbridge remains an important southern base. On 14 December 2017, No. 73109 (built in 1966 as E6015) is stabled there between duties.

Class 73 locos are regular visitors to Brush's workshops at Loughborough in order to receive attention. On 19 April 2017, Caledonian Sleeper-liveried No. 73971 heads south through Chesterfield on a light engine move from Edinburgh's Craigentinny depot, destined for the works. It was also built in 1966, as E6029.

The Brush Type 4, which was to become Class 47, was the most numerous class of main line diesel in BR days. With over 500 examples built, a few remain in various operators' hands and are registered for use across the UK rail network. One such example is No. 47810, then owned by DRS and seen here at their Crewe Gresty Bridge depot on 19 July 2014. It was originally numbered D1924 when built at the end of 1965 and is currently owned by Arlington Fleet Services at Eastleigh.

A number of Class 47 examples were re-built at the turn of the millennium and re-designated as Class 57. On 1 October 2017, No. 57301 was also to be found at DRS's Crewe base. This loco was originally built in January 1965 and numbered D1653.

The use of Brush Type 2 locomotives on today's railway has all but ceased. Nevertheless, the popular Class 31 locos were built between 1957 and 1962 and a number of examples reached their half centuries. Until recently Network Rail used four examples on their test trains, including No. 31105, which is seen here at Derby on 5 December 2017. It was originally numbered D5523 when built in 1959.

On 9 February 2015, another Network Rail example, numbered No. 31233, is seen passing through Loughborough at the head of a test train from Derby to Hither Green. It was built in October 1960 and numbered D5660 when new.

Here are a couple of examples of Class 37 locos nearing the end of their days. First, former DRS-owned No. 37603 is seen stored at Derby on 5 May 2017. It started life back in May 1962 as D6739.

Secondly, Network Rail's yellow example, No. 37198, has recently been moved to the same Derby complex. It is believed that it will be used as a 'parts donor' in order to keep NR's fleet of four Class 97s (derivatives from Class 37s) in traffic. It was seen there on 16 February 2018.

Over 200 Class 20s were built over a ten-year period in the 1950s and 1960s. In addition to their autumn leaf-fall duties with DRS, several GBRf members of the class continue to be gainfully employed on the movement of London Underground stock around the network, working as two pairs in top and tail formation. On 20 March 2013, No. 20096 (originally numbered D8096 when built in 1961) is nearest the camera as the combination passes through Burton upon Trent. Its sister loco at this end is No. 20107.

On 21 September 2017, No. 20107 is captured again, waiting alongside Derby station. This loco was also built at the end of 1961 and was numbered D8107 on delivery.

The Class 20s that appear on GBRf's London Underground stock moves carry a variety of liveries. Both are seen at Derby on 15 December 2014 on one such working. No. 20132, named *Barrow Hill Depot*, was built in 1966 as D8132.

Sister machine No. 20118, named *Saltburn-by-the-Sea*, was built four years earlier in 1962 and numbered D8118. Both these locos carry the Railfreight livery of grey bodysides, yellow cabs and a white double arrow. This loco also carries the Thornaby depot 'kingfisher' logo.

The West Coast Railway Company (WCRC) still has four Class 33 locos on its books. They occasionally move between the company's two sites at Carnforth (north Lancashire) and Southall, in West London. On 3 June 2013, No. 33029 heads through Nuneaton on a southbound light engine move between the two. This machine was built in March 1961 and was delivered new as D6547.

On 4 December 2017, sister loco No. 33207 is seen in the company of another of WCRC's veterans, No. 47245. They are working a short rake of coaching stock from Arlington Fleet Services at Eastleigh to their Carnforth base. They are seen coming off the curve into Coventry station. No. 33207 was new in March 1962 as D6592 while No. 47245 was delivered in December 1965 and originally carried the number D1922.

Several Class 57s carried Network Rail yellow livery and four are seen in this view of Eastleigh Works on 30 August 2013. No. 57301 is seen to the left of Nos 57312 and 57305, with a partial view of No. 57306 to the side.

On 20 May 2014, No. 57312 was still in Network Rail yellow when seen at Water Orton on a DRS working from Crewe to Bescot and Toton. Numbered D1811, it was delivered in February 1965.

If you are looking for Class 73s then Tonbridge is a good place to start, as demonstrated by this view across the town's West Yard on 25 June 2016. With No. 73212 *Fiona* in the foreground, a total of eight members of the class can be seen in this shot. This loco was newly delivered in October 1965 as E6008.

No. 73212 is also seen on the rear of this working viewed on 13 October 2015. Sister machine No. 73138 is at the business end of this Tonbridge to Derby Network Rail test train as it heads north through Market Harborough. No. 73138 was delivered in October 1966 as E6045.

The Network Rail-owned shunter No. 08417 also carries its yellow colour and can usually be seen in the rail complex at Derby. It is seen between duties on 2 February 2017. This loco dates back to July 1958, when it carried the number D3532.

Across the running lines at nearby Etches Park, East Midlands Trains No. 08899 can be seen on 6 October 2016. It is named *Midland Railway Company 175 – 1829 to 2014*. It was one of the last of these shunters to be built, being delivered in May 1962 as D4129. These days it rarely leaves its Derby base.

On 4 September 2017, two of DRS's veteran Class 37s worked back to their Crewe Gresty Bridge depot from Old Oak Common, with No. 37218 leading the pairing. This loco was delivered new in January 1964 as D6918.

No. 37069 was on the rear as they headed north through Nuneaton. This machine is eighteen months older than No. 37218, its sister loco. It was built in July 1962 as D6769.

Until recently Colas had a small fleet of thee Class 47s; these have now been sold to GBRf. One of these machines, No. 47739 *Robin of Templecombe*, was seen being dragged through Tamworth High Level on 28 June 2017. Back in August 1964, this loco was delivered new as D1615. In this picture, Class 70 No. 70801 is providing the power on the move from Washwood Heath to Barrow Hill depot.

On 17 December 2017, Colas used another of its Class 47s for route learning duties on South Humberside. No. 47727 *Rebecca* is seen passing through Barnetby station (before the semaphore signalling was replaced) on a circular from the oil terminal at nearby Lindsey. Also built in 1964, it was delivered in October that year as D1629.

The Class 50s were built between 1967 and 1968, and therefore just qualify for inclusion in this publication. Fifty Class 50 locos were built and a third of these survived into preservation. Several of these are main line registered and find use across the network, being hired in by various operators. On 18 May 2015, No. 50007 *Hercules* leads a pair on a light engine move through Rugby station. This loco was built in March 1968 as D407.

Its partner on this rainy day in Rugby was Network SouthEast-liveried No. 50017 *Royal Oak*. It was delivered in April 1968 as D417. The pair had arrived on a light engine move from Washwood Heath.

On 22 September 2017, sister loco No. 50008 *Thunderer* was to be found on a circular working to and from Derby. It is seen during a layover at Stafford station. This machine was also new in March 1968 and was numbered D417 when delivered.

Another Class 50, No. 50049 *Defiance*, was stabled at Derby station on 8 March 2018. It was used for route learning for those operators affected by the station blockade diversions scheduled to commence in July 2018. This machine was the last of the class to be built. It was new in December 1968 as D449.

For several years DRS have operated a civil engineer's working linking Crewe and Bescot yards. This working often continued from there to and from Toton. In 2014, their veteran Class 57/0 machines were often used, working in pairs. On 30 June that year, No. 57012 leads No. 57008 through Tamworth High Level, heading for Toton. No. 57012 was delivered in July 1965 as D1854.

On 22 July 2014, it was the turn of No. 57009 to partner No. 57008. This time the location is Water Orton. No. 57009 was built in February 1965 as D1664.

Two DRS machines with contrasting futures are to be found at Derby on 6 December 2017. The unnumbered Class 37 on the left will carry number 37407 when the work on it is completed. Its immediate future is secure, as can be seen later in this publication. The fate of No. 37409 on the right is less clear. It was in store when this picture was taken. It emerged as D6970 when new in March 1965.

Another Class 37 that achieved celebrity status prior to its disposal is No. 37670. It was out-shopped in DB red back in 2009 and since then it has had several owners and has been dragged to several locations. On 13 March 2017, it was to be found at the former depot complex at Leicester as a stored loco owned by Europhoenix. It has since lost its bogies. Back in October 1963 it was newly delivered as D6882.

The former depot area at Leicester is also home to other examples of our '50 not out' club. The distinctively liveried No. 37670 can be seen in this shot taken a few weeks earlier on 3 February 2017, prior to it being shunted to the front of this loco line-up. On that day another Europhoenix example, No. 37510, leads the stored line. This machine also dates back to 1963 and was new as D6812 in February of that year.

On 16 November 2016, the depot area was also home to No. 37906. This UK Rail Leasing-owned machine was transferred here in 2015. No. 37906, built in 1963, emerged in November that year as D6906.

Two veteran Class 73s can often be seen within the RTC complex at Derby on 5 January 2018. No. 73139 is owned by Loram and is, in effect, a static advertisement for their services. It now sports a livery offering 'Repair – Re-engineer – Repaint'. This electro-diesel was delivered new as E6046 in October 1966.

Derby is also home to celebrity-liveried No. 73101. This loco, carrying (faded) Pullman livery, has languished here for many years. Remarkably, it still carries its name, *The Royal Alex*. As mentioned in the introduction, I retain an affection for this particular loco; it remains one of the most noteworthy sightings I have witnessed through Northampton station over the last fifty years.

Despite a substantial fleet of more modern locos on their books, Freightliner Class 86s can be seen daily on the WCML container trains south of Crewe. On 12 May 2015, No. 86609 leads a Tilbury to Crewe Freightliner through Nuneaton. It was built fifty years earlier, in August 1965, as E3174.

On 10 January 2017, Nos 86605 and 86614 are entrusted with a run on the Down fast as they head north through Nuneaton with a Felixstowe to Ditton working. No. 86605 was delivered new as E3185 in October 1965, with No. 86614 following in March 1966 as E3145.

On 17 June 2014, No. 86627 (with No. 86609) heads south on the WCML at Nuneaton with a Ditton to Felixstowe working. No. 86609 was built in July 1966 as E3159.

Another southbound working is seen through Nuneaton on 19 January 2016, being hauled by No. 86632 (with No. 86627). This time the Felixstowe-bound container train originated from Trafford Park. No. 86632 was delivered new as E3148 in April 1966 while No. 86627 was built in June the previous year as E3110.

For many years Network Rail test trains were in the hands of DRS Class 37s. These locos either worked in pairs in top and tail mode or singly, with a Driving Brake control car. On 3 February 2017, No. 37667 is returning to NR's Derby base; on this occasion the working had started that morning from Bristol Temple Meads. This loco was built at English Electric's Vulcan Foundry in July 1963 and was numbered D6851.

On 22 June 2016, No. 37602 (with No. 37609 on the rear) is returning from Tonbridge to Derby via the Midland Main Line when photographed at Bedford. It was built in November 1962 as D6782.

On 7 September 2017, the tranquillity of the Norfolk countryside is interrupted by a pair of DRS Class 37s approaching Brundall Gardens. Short sets of loco-hauled coaching stock have been used to supplement the local fleet of diesel units between Norwich and Great Yarmouth. In this view, No. 37716 leads the 13.40 train from Great Yarmouth into the station. This loco entered traffic back in February 1963 as D6794.

At the rear of this working is No. 37405. This machine dates back to May 1965 and was numbered D6794 when delivered.

First Great Western maintains a small pool of four Class 57s for its overnight sleeper services between Paddington and Penzance. On 31 May 2016, No. 57604 *Pendennis Castle* calls at Par station with the Paddington-bound service. The loco was new as D1859 when delivered in August 1965.

A couple of days earlier, sister loco No. 57605 *Totnes Castle* was pressed into service to rescue a failed CrossCountry HST on 29 May. Summoned from Penzance to the Newquay branch, it is seen dragging the set (with power car No. 43378 at the head) towards Par station. This loco also dates from August 1965 and carried the number D1856 when new.

The leaf-fall season was almost at an end on 14 December 2017 in these views taken at Tonbridge's West Yard. A number of GBRf's fleet of Class 73s find work on these services. No. 73119 *Borough of Eastleigh* was not required that day and remained in the yard. It was delivered in March 1966 as E6025.

Sister No. 73136 *Mhairi* was also out of action that day. This machine is six months younger, and carried the number E6043 when delivered in September 1966.

The pairing of No. 73141 *Charlotte* and No. 73128 *OVS Bulleid CBE Southern Railway* were more gainfully employed and are seen about to leave the yard on a 'Tonbridge Circular'. Both are 1966-built locos with No. 73141 appearing in December that year as E6048 and No. 73128 a few months earlier, in June, as E6035.

Another pair, Nos 73213 *Rhodalyn* and 73201 *Broadlands*, were also getting ready for service that day. No. 73213 was built in February 1966 as E6018 while No. 73201 was the last built of the fifty machines, appearing in January 1967 as E6049.

A few shunting locos are still in use in Scotland. In Inverness, the Anglo-Scottish sleeper stock is released from the platform by one of the depot's resident shunters. Here on 4 April 2015, No. 08523 moves the Caledonian Sleeper coaches on to the depot for servicing. No. 08523, as D3685, was built in September 1958.

Further south, No. 08472 is seen on 6 October 2017 at Edinburgh's Craigentinny depot. It finds employment shunting coaching stock within the depot complex. This shunter was also built in 1958, appearing in November that year as D3587.

DRS's ageing fleet of Class 20s can still occasionally be seen around the network despite the continual threat that 'this year will be their last'. No. 20303 *Max Joule 1958–1999* was built as D8127 in July 1962 and had therefore already clocked up a half century when pictured here stabled at Doncaster on 24 March 2014.

On 19 July 2014, No. 20309 was to be found on Crewe Gresty Bridge depot. This machine is even older, having been built as D8075 back in July 1961.

A pair of WCRC Class 57s was used to haul a rake of charter stock from Carnforth to Ely on 23 June 2017. No. 57313 leads this top and tail working south through Doncaster station. This loco started life as D1890 in July 1965.

Bringing up the rear was No. 57316. This WCRC machine was new in March 1966, numbered D1992.

DRS Class 37s have been a regular sight on Network Rail test trains for a number of years. On 14 September 2015, No. 37604 leaves Oxford following a signal check, working from Derby to Eastleigh. This loco is one of the oldest members of the original class, having been built in February 1961 as D6707.

The Midland Main Line is the routing for this Network Rail test train from Derby to Hither Green. On 28 March 2014, No. 37610 is seen approaching Wellingborough. At the time this picture was taken it carried the name *TS (Ted) Cassady 14.5.61 – 6.4.08*. It was delivered in October 1963 as D6881.

On 20 June 2017, two of Network Rail's yellow-liveried Class 73s are seen heading through Nuneaton. No. 73951 *Malcolm Brinded* leads the pair on a Northampton to Derby light engine move. This loco entered traffic in October 1965 as E6010.

On the rear is sister loco No. 73952 *Janis Kong*. This loco was built in February 1966 as E6019.

The popularity of the veteran Class 37s has been enhanced by the appearance of DRS examples in BR blue with large logos. On 13 March 2015, an immaculate No. 37401 is seen at Derby. In February 1965, the loco was delivered as D6968.

On 14 April 2016, No. 37403 is also seen at Derby. This time the loco is captured in the final stages of its finishing. It already carries its *Isle of Mull* nameplate, but it is awaiting the number '403' and the large logo double arrow. This loco was built towards the end of the production run and emerged as D6607 in October 1965.

It has taken a little longer for No. 37407 to make its large logo re-emergence. It is seen here on 9 March 2018 with saloon *Caroline*. The pair are heading to Kettering for a couple of return trips on the line from there to Corby. Another loco to emerge in October 1965, No. 37407 was originally numbered D6605.

No. 37025 *Inverness TMD* is another example of a Class 37 out-shopped in BR blue with large logos. This time the work was carried out by the Scottish 37 Group and the Bo'ness Diesel Group. It found main line work on 26 June 2017 when propelling a test train from Rugby back to Derby. It is seen here at Nuneaton and will reverse at Lichfield. It was built in August 1961 as D6725.

There was more charter train action for DRS's Class 57s on 9 June 2017. Originally built in February 1966 as D1931, No. 57316 *Pride of Crewe* leads a Preston to Chesterfield working through Nuneaton.

On the rear is No. 57307 *Lady Penelope*. This batch of Class 57/3 locos are perhaps best known for their rescue duties on the main line network, earning the nickname 'Thunderbirds'. No. 57307 retains its original name. It emerged new in September 1965 as D1901.

On 3 July 2017, the colourful pairing of green-liveried No. 37057 and Colas-liveried No. 37116 were in charge of a Derby to Eastleigh test train. No. 37116 leads the working south through Bedford. It dates back to March 1963, when it was delivered new as D6816.

BR style green-liveried No. 37057 is found on the rear of the working. It was built in October 1962 as D6757.

On 2 March 2015, WCRC No. 57315 heads east through Acton Main Line and on to the North London Line with an empty stock working. This machine dates back to October 1965 and was numbered D1911 when new.

The same loco was called upon for a loco move on 3 December 2013 with stablemate No. 57601. The pair dragged Nos 56031, 56069 and 56106 to Leicester. They are seen here dragging the trio of Class 56s, which themselves built much more recently (between 1977 and 1982), into the Leicester depot complex for further storage. No. 57601 started life as D1759 in August 1964.

ROG's Class 37s are in demand for a variety of stock moves across the country. On 11 July 2017, No. 37884 is seen passing through Rugby dragging two displaced Class 319 units, Nos 319012 and 319215, from Hornsey to Long Marston for storage. The Class 37 first appeared as D6883 in November 1963.

Sister loco No. 37800 is slightly older, having first appeared some six months earlier as D6843 in May 1963. On 14 July 2017, it is seen heading north through Milton Keynes Central dragging a newly delivered Mobile Maintenance Train.

WCRC No. 47786 was built in April 1964 as D1730. Shortly after its fiftieth birthday, the loco is seen on 21 September 2014 on the rear of an empty stock working from Norwich to the company's northern base at Carnforth. The train is passing Marholm, just north of Peterborough.

The same location sees a second fifty-year-old veteran loco on 30 November 2014. Built in September 1964 as D1617, No. 47760 is found on the rear of another empty stock working back to Carnforth. On this occasion the stock had originated at Ely. No. 57313 is leading the train.

These two photographs feature DRS Class 37s that date back to 1962. No. 37038 was built in May 1962 as D6738. It is seen here on 30 March 2017 leading No. 37716 through Tamworth on a mixed rake of coaching stock from Arlington Fleet Services at Eastleigh to Nemesis Rail at Burton-on-Trent.

Sister loco No. 37059 was built in October 1962 as D6759. It was entrusted with a much lighter load on 3 February 2015, as it is seen arriving at Doncaster with a single Greater Anglia coach that it had hauled from their depot at Crown Point, Norwich.

A pair of Freightliner Class 86s head south through Tamworth on 8 May 2017. No. 86608, built in March 1966 as E3140, leads No. 86622 on a Trafford Park to Felixstowe working. This loco enjoyed life as a one-off for a number of years as uniquely re-geared No. 86501.

No. 86622 is the second loco in this photograph, while No. 86604 leads the pairing through Bletchley on an Ipswich to Crewe container train on 25 May 2017. No. 86604 was newly delivered in August 1965 as E3103.

DRS No. 37424 has something of a double identity. This large logo machine was named *Avro Vulcan XH558* in July 2016. At the same time, the number 37558 was applied to its sides. With '424' showing on the cab end, the loco heads light engine southbound through Leyland, near Preston, on 1 October 2017. The loco was built in May 1965 as D6979.

Class 37 No. 37425 *Sir Robert McAlpine/Concrete Bob* was also built in 1965, entering traffic in July that year as D6992. On 11 November 2017, it is found at the head of a stock move from Norwich to Bounds Green that involved several Greater Anglia coaches and fellow DRS locos Nos 57010, 47805 and 47818.

Until recently, DRS's Class 20s were still regular performers on nuclear flask traffic to and from Sellafield, as this 2013 photograph demonstrates. On 17 June 2013, No. 20302 (with Nos 20304 and 37423) leads a triple-headed return working from Seaham to their Cumbrian base. The trio are seen passing the Tyne and Wear Metro station at Pelaw. No. 20302 was built in September 1961 as D8084.

In the autumn of the same year, No. 20308 waits at the head of an RHTT working with No. 20304 at the far end of the train. The pair are captured between duties in Sheffield station. No. 20308 was built as D8196 in February 1967.

WCRC's fleet of Class 47s is frequently seen on coaching stock moves on the West Coast Main Line. These trains usually operate to and from their base at Carnforth. On 8 May 2017, No. 47237 heads north through Nuneaton with a rake of coaches from Southall. No. 47237 entered service as D1914 in November 1965.

On 15 April 2016, No. 47851 heads in the opposite direction on the rear of an empty coaching stock move from Carnforth to Norwich. This loco was built in January 1965 and was numbered D1648 when new.

Derby station often sees loco convoys operated by DRS. On 21 July 2016, two such moves occurred within a few hours of each other. First, No. 37606 arrived at the head of a convoy from Crewe. The other locos were Nos 37612, 68005 and 68022. No. 37606 was delivered in January 1963 as D6790.

Later that day, No. 37612 returned to Derby at the head of a five-loco convoy that also involved Nos 20303, 20305, 37424 and 37606. The locos were working from Barrow Hill to Crewe. DRS No. 37612 was also built in 1963 and carried the number D6879 when delivered in October that year.

These two photographs demonstrate that DRS's Class 57s are found from one end of the country to the other. First, on 2 October 2017, No. 57304 *Pride of Cheshire* is found alongside the 'wall' at Carlisle station. This loco was built at Crewe as D1639 in December 1964.

At the other end of England a few months earlier, on 29 April, No. 57303 *Pride of Carlisle* is found outside the former works complex at Eastleigh. This loco emerged from Brush Traction in Loughborough as D1957 in January 1967.

The workshops at Loughborough have, much more recently, been responsible for rebuilding six Class 73 locomotives for the Anglo-Scottish Caledonian Sleeper service. Two of these Class 73/9s, Nos 73967 and 73968, are glimpsed from the adjacent field on 3 November 2015. No. 73968 was originally numbered E6023 when built in March 1966, while No. 73967 was one of the original batch of six locos built. It dates from November 1962, when it was numbered E6006.

On 14 October 2017, No. 73970 has just arrived at the West Highland sleeper destination of Fort William. The driver is about to propel the stock out of the platform to enable the loco to run-round. It was originally delivered in November 1965 as E6009.

Two Colas Class 37 workings on test trains from the former Southern Region were routed via the Midland Main Line within a couple of hours of each other on 8 September 2015. First, No. 37219 hauled a working from Hither Green back to Derby. As D6919, this loco was built in January 1964.

Two hours later, No. 37421 was at the business end of a return working from Tonbridge to Network Rail's Derby base. No. 37421 is a later example, built as D6967 in February 1965.

Sister loco No. 37175 fared less well on 13 June 2016. It was not long into its southbound journey to Hither Green when it developed a train fault. The consist is seen here recessed adjacent to Leicester station. This 1963 machine was built in September that year as D6875.

The versatile Colas Class 37s also find themselves working to many other parts of the country. On 29 June 2017, for example, No. 37254 finds itself in Doncaster West Yard between duties. This popular loco carried InterCity livery until it was repainted into Colas colours in April 2017 and named *Cardiff Canton*. It was newly delivered in January 1965 as D6954.

Most of the former British Rail(ways) diesel shunters found on the network today are classified as Class 08s. One exception is Arriva Traincare's No. 09204, which is seen here shunting in their Crewe complex on 24 March 2017. It carried the number 08717 for almost twenty years. Prior to that it was delivered new in May 1960 as D3884.

The fourteen Class 07 diesel shunters were originally built as steam engine replacements for shunting within Southampton Docks. It is therefore appropriate that No. 07007 has survived in the area and could be found working within the complex at Eastleigh Works on 30 August 2013. It started life as D2991 in July 1962.

On 13 October 2015, No. 37668 unusually found itself working solo on a rake of WCRC coaching stock being moved from Southall to Carnforth. It is heading north through Nuneaton shortly after passing its half century. As D6957, it was newly delivered in January 1965.

Sister WCRC loco No. 37716 found itself on lighter duties on 16 June 2015. It is seen here pausing at the east end of Acton Yard, fitted with recording equipment for use on the section of line between Kettering and Corby. This loco is one of the earliest members of the class, dating back to June 1961 when it was delivered as D6716.

The Class 20 survivors have sported a variety of distinctive liveries over the last few years. For example, on 30 June 2014, No. 20142 is seen between duties at Derby in Balfour Beatty colours. It was built in May 1966 as D8142.

Two years later, the same loco has been repainted into BR blue livery. It stands at the former Leicester depot with No. 20205 in the foreground. As D8305, No. 20205 was one of the last machines in a production run of well over 200 English Electric Type 1 locos, having been built in April 1967.

Another distinctive colour scheme is seen here on locos Nos 20314 and 20311. They both carry the orange and black colours of the Harry Needle Railroad Company. The two are pictured at Derby having just arrived from Banbury with the barrier vehicles used for the movement of London Underground stock. Both of these machines started their working lives in the Glasgow area. No. 20314 was delivered in February 1962 as D8117 and No. 20311 was delivered in December 1961 as D8102.

At the opposite end of this working is GBRf liveried No. 20905. This comparative youngster only reached its half century in 2018, having been built as D8325 in February 1968. It emerged almost at the end of the production run.

The Brush workshops at Loughborough also carried out conversions to five electro-diesels for GBRf which were re-designated Class 73/9s. They are primarily used on Network Rail related duties on the former Southern Region. One example, No. 73962 *Dick Mabbutt*, was heading in this direction when removed from its train on 9 January 2017. It was to be found languishing at the buffer stops north of Leicester station until recovery was effected a few days later. No. 73962 was built as E6032 in May 1966.

On 3 October 2015, No. 73963 *Janice* was found deep in Southern territory. It was in the company of other GBRf and Colas locos on Eastleigh stabling point. This loco was also delivered in May 1966 as E6030.

As already mentioned, Tonbridge is usually home to several class examples. On 25 June 2016, No. 73964 *Jeanette* was stabled here awaiting work. Another May 1966-built machine, No. 73964 was originally numbered E6031.

Four examples were to be found on one light engine move on 11 June 2015. Nearest the camera is No. 73961 *Alison* as the convoy heads north from Bedford with sister locos Nos 73962, 73963 and 73964. April 1966 saw No. 73961 enter traffic as E6026.

As mentioned earlier, the DRS Class 37s augment the ageing fleet of diesel units on the East Anglian branches. On 16 June 2016, *No. 37419 Carl Haviland 1954–2012* has just arrived at Norwich on a working from Great Yarmouth with No. 37422 on the rear. This loco was built towards the end of the production run in June 1965 as D6991.

The coaching stock from these workings is often returned to Crewe for attention and No. 37422 was involved on 4 December 2017, hauling the set northwards through Nuneaton with No. 57301 on the rear. No. 37422 was numbered D6966 when delivered in February 1965.

In 2016, Rail Operations Group expanded its loco fleet with the acquisition of several Class 47 machines. Two of these locos, Nos 47847 and 47848, were found stabled at Derby on 27 February 2017. No. 47847 was built in October 1964 as D1774.

ROG's No. 47848 is seen again on 8 June 2017; this time the venue is the former depot area at Leicester. This loco was built in January 1965 as D1652.

ROG's Class 47s are regular visitors to Ely, moving stock to and from the Potter Group base there, and on 20 July 2017 No. 47815 is seen in the yard. New as D1748, this loco was built in July 1964.

Another 1964-built machine, this time built in August that year as D1655, privately owned No. 47773 is found at Leicester depot on 4 March 2016.

Class 08 diesel shunters continue to be used at depots and workshops around the country, including at Wabtec, Doncaster. On 25 October 2017, No. 08853 shunts East Coast loco No. 91118. It dates back to June 1960, when it was delivered as D4021.

Moments earlier, sister machine No. 08669 is seen sitting at the 'throat' of Wabtec's complex. Also built in 1960 as D3836, this machine emerged a few months earlier, in January.

Two more examples of DRS's Class 57/0 machines are seen here. They were both built in January 1965. First, No. 57003, built as D1798, is seen on 9 December 2015 at Chester. It arrived on a light engine run from and to the company's Crewe Gresty Bridge depot.

Secondly, No. 57002 is seen in the company of Greater Anglia's No. 90002 (and a DBSO coach), heading through Nuneaton on a Crewe to Norwich move.

Two more veteran electric locos are used by GBRf on empty stock movements in connection with Caledonian Sleeper services. On 27 April 2017, No. 86101 *Sir William A. Stanier FRS* is stabled in Wembley Yard between duties.

Sister loco No. 86401 is also employed on these duties. Looking in need of a makeover, the electric is being dragged through Loughborough station on its way to Brush's workshops nearby to be outshopped for these duties.

Two veteran Class 31s, both over fifty years old, were in the hands of RMS Locotec while this book was written, albeit with an uncertain future as they were being offered for sale by tender. On 24 May 2015, No. 31601 *Devon Diesel Society* is seen heading eastbound through Exeter St Davids, working light engine from Totnes to Tyseley. This machine dates from April 1960 and was built as D5609.

Sister loco D5809 was built in July 1961. It is seen over half a century later as No. 31452 (in the company of No. 50008), adjacent to Derby station.

Veteran Class 37s were in action in the north of Scotland on 4 April 2015. No. 37607 is seen leading No. 37218 on the Inverness to Kyle of Lochalsh leg of a railtour. The pair are approaching Dingwall. No. 37607 entered traffic as D6803 in January 1964.

On 4 January 2018, No. 37423 *Spirit of the Lakes* finds itself passing through Nuneaton on the rear of a Crewe to Norwich stock move, involving a single coach and with No. 37609 leading. No. 37423 was another example to be built towards the end of production, appearing as D6996 in July 1965.

Two more DRS Class 37s are seen in action here and in the Crewe area. First, built as D6959 in January 1965, No. 37259 is seen at Crewe station on 14 March 2014 on an infrastructure working.

Just across town, No. 37609 is found on 1 October 2017 at Gresty Bridge depot. The loco is seen from the familiar 'slope' at the entrance. Built as D6813, the loco dates from February 1963.

These two shots involve two more of First Great Western's (FGW) sleeper Class 57s. No. 57603 *Tintagel Castle* was delivered back in March 1965 as D1830. It is seen here heading south through Bedford, returning to Old Oak Common depot in West London after receiving attention at Derby.

Stablemate No. 57602 *Restormel Castle* was built a month earlier as D1818. It is seen here on FGW's 'Old Oak' depot from a train passing on the Great Western main line.

WCRC Class 47s are often involved in providing 'insurance' for steam-hauled charters. On 25 June 2016, No. 47580 *County of Essex* is found on the rear of one such northbound working through Bedford. Built in September 1964, the loco was then numbered D1762.

Six months later at the same location, No. 47854 *Diamond Jubilee* is on the rear of an Ealing Broadway to York charter. The stock is being hauled by No. 46233 *Duchess of Sutherland*. The Class 47 was built in November 1965 as D1972.

DRS Class 57 'Thunderbirds' are regularly stabled at Crewe station in case they are called upon to rescue a failure. On 22 September 2017 it was the turn of No. 57311 *Thunderbird* to perform these duties. It was delivered in August 1964 and originally carried the number D1611.

These locos are sometimes called upon to rescue a service operated by a company other than Virgin Trains. On 6 January 2015, DRS sister loco No. 57302 *Chad Varah* was summoned from nearby Rugby to rescue one of their own services. A Class 66-hauled Daventry to Coatbridge intermodal service had ground to a halt in Nuneaton station platform, and No. 57302 took the entire consist forward to Crewe. New as D1928, this loco was built in January 1966.

A handful of Class 08 shunters remain in use by the major freight operating companies, including Freightliner at their base at Southampton Maritime. On 30 April 2017, a Bank Holiday, their own No. 08785 was stabled out of use. This veteran was built in April 1960 as D3953.

Sister loco No. 08873 was also stabled here on the same day. It is seen outside Freightliner's maintenance depot. This machine was delivered in November 1960 as D4041.

On 21 April 2016, No. 86613 leads No. 86614 through Bletchley. The pair are heading north on a Felixstowe to Trafford Park Freightliner having taken over haulage of this service at Ipswich. No. 86613 was built in November 1965 and was originally numbered E3128.

Another northbound pair of Class 86s are seen a couple of miles further north on 26 June 2015. No. 86638 leads No. 86612 through Milton Keynes Central station at the head of a Tilbury to Crewe Freightliner. No. 86638 was delivered in June 1965 as E3108.

Class 86s can often be seen on local light engine movements between the various yards and depots in the Crewe area. On 26 October 2017, No. 86612 is seen in the company of No. 90045 on one such working. The Class 86 was built in September 1965 as E3122.

Most of the surviving Class 86s are owned and operated by Freightliner. Privately owned No. 86259, seen here on 19 February 2018 at Rugby, is an exception. It has been restored to its original blue and white colours and carries a different nameplate on each bodyside, namely *Peter Pan* and *Les Ross*. It also carries its original style number plate, E3137. It was built in January 1966.

The remaining Class 47s can be seen far and wide across the network as these four views demonstrate. On 4 October 2017, WCRC No. 47804 was at the head of a returning charter from Fort William to Kettering. This loco was built in October 1965 as D1965. A photograph of No. 37669 on the rear of this train is found towards the front of this publication.

At the other end of the country, No. 47818 is seen within the works complex at Eastleigh on 29 April 2017, with a mixture of stock for company. This loco was newly delivered as D1917 in December 1965.

On 18 September 2015, Freightliner's celebrity Class 47, No. 47830, was involved in a long-distance light engine move. It is seen here arriving at Bedford, working from Leeds to Eastleigh. New as D1645, the loco was built in December 1964.

Another long-distance Class 47 'drag' took place on 10 October 2016. A GBRf Class 66 took No. 47853, which was built in June 1964 as D1733, from Carlisle to Barrow Hill. The duo is seen passing through Derby.

The remaining twenty or so active members of Class 57 continue to be used on a variety of duties. On 1 November 2016, DRS No. 57308, then named *County of Staffordshire*, is engaged on 'Thunderbird' rescue duties at the southern end of the WCML. It is seen here stabled in Wembley Yard. This loco was built in April 1965 as D1677.

On 4 May 2017, No. 57305 *Northern Princess* is seen arriving at Crewe with a rake of coaching stock that it has worked from Kidderminster. This veteran machine was built in May 1964 as D1758.

On 14 July 2017, No. 57306 *Her Majesty's Railway Inspectorate 175* was called on to 'drag' a pair of Class 37s, Nos 37602 and 37606, from Crewe to Burton-on-Trent (Nemesis Rail). The trio are approaching their destination as they pass through Burton station. No. 57306 was delivered new as D1919 in November 1965.

On 29 August 2015, No. 57310 *Pride of Cumbria* was involved in another 'drag'. This time the 57 was used by ROG to drag South Eastern unit No. 375303 from Ramsgate to Derby. They are seen here at Bedford. No. 57310 was built in September 1964 and was numbered D1618.

Another trio of DRS veterans is seen heading through Chesterfield on 24 March 2014. No. 47501 *Craftsman* leads Nos 37059 and 20301 on a Crewe to Barrow Hill light engine move. The Class 47 was built as D1964 and delivered in June 1966.

With No. 20301 on the rear of this convoy, it provides a rare view of a Class 20 showing its nose end. This loco was built in November 1959 as D8047.

A small pool of four former Class 37 locos were placed in a Network Rail Class 97/3 subclass. On 23 April 2015, No. 97301 is seen at the head of a test train. It was originally built as D6800 in December 1962.

At least two of these machines can usually be found on RHTT workings during the autumn leaf-fall season. No. 97302 is seen at Crewe station, where the train will reverse, on 4 December 2014. This loco entered service in August 1963 as D6870.

On 21 September 2017, No. 97303 is nearest the camera when seen top and tailing a test train at Derby. No. 97301 is on the other end. No. 97303 was built in October 1963 as D6878.

The next day the pairing had changed. No. 97304 *John Tiley* (with No. 97301 for company) arrives at Crewe on 22 September on a light engine move from Derby. No. 97304 was new as D6917 when built in January 1964.

On 22 May 2017, GBRf duo No. 73107 *Tracy* and No. 73965 were seen at Nuneaton being 'dragged' by No. 66771 on a light engine move from the Severn Valley Railway back to Eastleigh. No. 73107 was built as E6013 in December 1965.

A few months later, No. 73965 is seen again on a light engine move on 25 October. It is on the rear of the convoy passing through Conisbrough, South Yorkshire, with Caledonian Sleeper examples Nos 73966 and 73971 for company. The three locos were on a Loughborough Brush to Edinburgh Craigentinny move. No. 73965, which was built in April 1966 as E6028, will be removed on arrival at Doncaster.

First Great Western continues to use diesel shunters within its depot complexes. On 28 September 2016, No. 08483 is seen at its Old Oak Common base when passing on the Great Western main line. No. 08483 was built in October 1958 as D3598.

On 28 May 2017, No. 08644 is found in one of their western outposts as it rests between shunting duties at Plymouth's Laira depot. This loco was built in February 1959 as D3811.

These two photographs show examples of two different classes of veteran machines that have survived into the 2010s. First, BR green-liveried No. 40012 *Aureol* (built as D212 and still carrying its original number) is seen at Barrow Hill on 10 November 2013. It was built in June 1959.

On 3 May 2014, a neglected No. 26011 can be seen from passing trains as it languishes within the Nemesis Rail yard at Burton-on-Trent. The former Scottish machine was built in January 1959 as D5311.

It is still possible to see loco movements on the main BR network that involve heritage traction convoys to and from preserved railways across the country. On 8 September 2016, No. 46045 (still carrying original number D182) is at the head of a trio of locos stabled adjacent to Derby station. The Peak was built in September 1962.

Its partners that day were No. 20059 and, nearest the camera, No. 20188. This loco also carries its original BR number, D8188, and was built back in January 1967.

On 7 June 2016, an immaculate Crompton, No. 33035, was on the rear of a convoy seen heading through Nuneaton that day. It was involved in a move from Didcot Railway Centre to Nene Valley Railway's headquarters at Peterborough. It entered service as D6553 in May 1961.

Another move through Nuneaton on 22 May 2017 saw No. 31271 *Stratford 1840–2001* being dragged by Deltic No. 55022. It, too, was heading for the Nene Valley Railway on a move from Washwood Heath (near Birmingham). No. 31271 was built in June 1961 as D5801.

A brightly coloured livery (Europhoenix) and a seemingly bright future is surely in store for these two veteran Class 37s. First, No. 37608 *Andromeda* is seen at the head of a test train at Derby on 22 February 2017. The loco was numbered D6722 when built in July 1961.

Secondly, No. 37601 *Perseus* is preparing to leave Leicester on 23 October 2017. It was built some six months earlier than No. 37608, in January 1961, as D6705.

18 July 2016 saw two more '50 not out' engines at Leicester. Deltic No. 55002 *The King's Own Yorkshire Light Infantry* is seen alongside No. 37350 as they prepare to reverse on to Leicester stabling point. They had arrived as a light engine move from Leeds. The Deltic was built in March 1961 as D9002 while No. 37350 dates from December 1960 as D6700, being the first loco of this class to be built.

Finally, I am sure we all have a favourite livery and this is one of mine. On 5 July 2013, loco No. 20189 sports its London Transport colours as it, appropriately, arrives at Leicester on a London Underground stock move. This machine entered service in January 1967 as D8189.